S0-EGS-697

Ice Cream Party

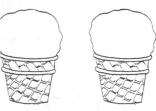

1. Brainstorm to list all the types of ice cream your students can think of. Have each student take one ice cream cone pattern and color it to represent the flavor of ice cream he/she likes best. (Reproduce the ice cream patterns on the next page.)
2. Make a large graph on butcher paper. Record the results by having your students pin or paste their ice cream cones in the correct column.

Which flavor of ice cream do you like best?

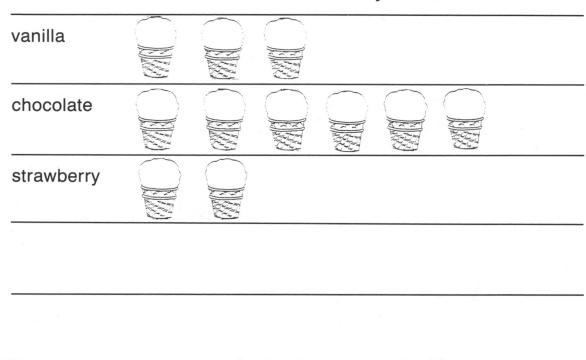

You may want to place all unusual or seldom-picked flavors in an "others" category.

3. Read the graph to find the answers to questions such as:
   a. How many different flavors did the class choose from?
   b. Which flavor did the most children choose?
   c. Which flavor was picked the least?
   d. Did more or less people choose your favorite flavor?
   e. Was there a flavor on the graph that no one picked?

NOTE: You may have your students fill in their own graphs using the form on page 3.

 Graphs

Patterns for Ice Cream Cones

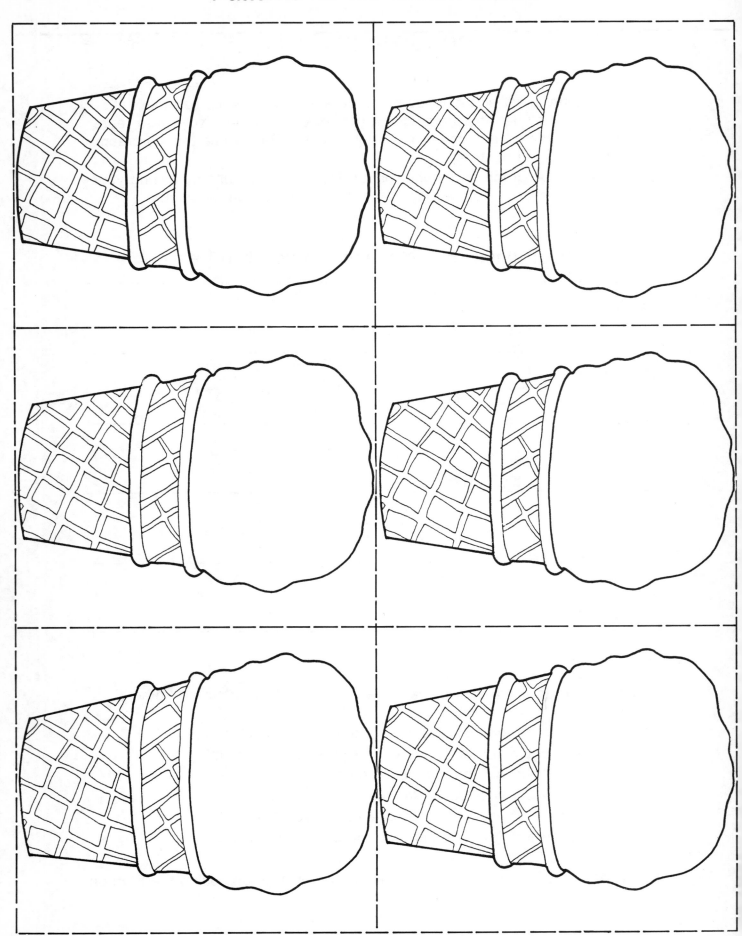

2

Graphs

Which flavor of ice cream do you like best?

Draw ice cream cones to show how many boys and girls chose each flavor.

vanilla	
chocolate	
strawberry	

3   Graphs

How do you get to school?

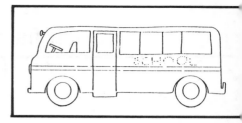

1. Brainstorm to list the ways students and teachers might use to get to school. List the types of transportation (or put up pictures) on the chalkboard.
2. Reproduce the patterns on the next page. (You will need several copies.) Have students select the picture that illustrates their means of transportation to school.
3. Make a large graph on butcher paper. Record the results by having students pin or paste their pictures in the correct columns.

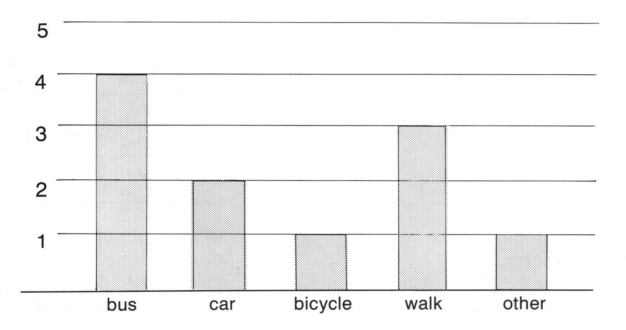

4. Read the graph to answer questions such as:
    a. How many children come to school by _____?
        bus _____   car _____
        bicycle _____   walk _____
    b. How many children come to school some other way? (You may want to have them recall some of these ways even though they are not shown on the graph.)
    c. Name the way most children in your class get to school.
    d. How many children come to school on four wheels? On two?
    e. What is the total number of children who ride to school?

NOTE: You may have your students fill in their own graph using the form on page 6.

Patterns for "How do you get to school?" Graph

 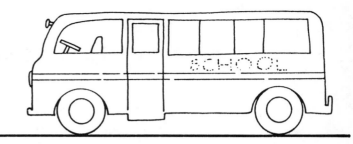

How do you get to school?

Color one box for each answer. Start at box one in each row.

	bus	car	bicycle	walk	other
15					
14					
13					
12					
11					
10					
9					
8					
7					
6					
5					
4					
3					
2					
1					

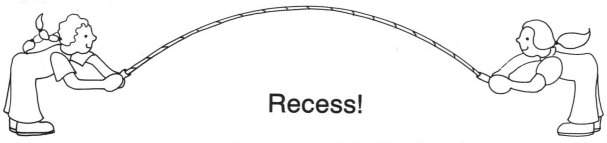

Recess!

1. Brainstorm to list types of activities children can do at recess. List these activities on the chalkboard.
2. Have each student come to the board and make a slash mark by his/her favorite recess activity.
3. Make a large graph on butcher paper. Record the results in line graph form. If your students are not ready for line graphs, make a bar graph instead.

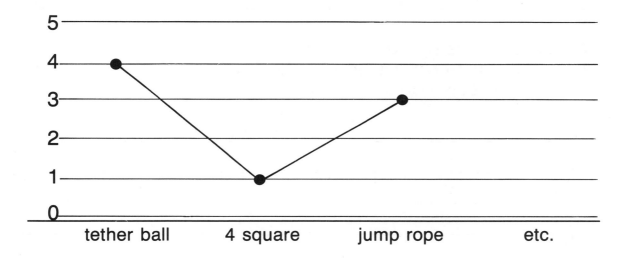

4. Read the graph to answer questions such as:
   a. How many different activities did we list on this graph?
   b. Which activity did the most students choose?
   c. Is there an activity that no one chose?
   d. Which activity did the smallest number of students choose?
   e. Did anyone choose an indoor activity for recess fun?

NOTE: You may have your students make a line graph of their own using the form on page 8. Have each child list three recess activities on his/her graph. Then ask 12 other students to choose which one of the activities they would like to play at recess. After the answers have been collected, have the students complete the line graph at the bottom of the page.

           Graphs

What do you like to do at recess?

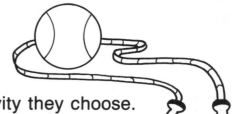

Make a mark for each boy or girl by the activity they choose.

1.

2.

3.

4. None of these.

Count the marks by each activity.
Put dots by the right numbers on the graph.
Connect the dots with straight lines.

```
12 ─────────────────────────────────────
11 ─────────────────────────────────────
10 ─────────────────────────────────────
 9 ─────────────────────────────────────
 8 ─────────────────────────────────────
 7 ─────────────────────────────────────
 6 ─────────────────────────────────────
 5 ─────────────────────────────────────
 4 ─────────────────────────────────────
 3 ─────────────────────────────────────
 2 ─────────────────────────────────────
 1 ─────────────────────────────────────

   1. _____   2. _____   3. _____   4. None of these
```

8   Graphs

Make a class graph.

In which month were you born?

1. Collecting information:
   Write the months of the year on the chalkboard. Have your students make a slash mark next to the name of the months in which they were born.
2. Make a large graph on butcher paper. Record the results in line graph form. (If your students are not ready for line graphs, make a bar graph instead.)

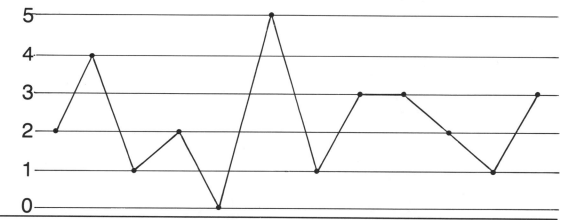

3. Read the graph to answer questions such as:
   a. How can you find information on a line graph?
   b. How many children were born in _____?
   c. In which month were the most children born?
   d. In which month were the fewest children born?
   e. Were more children born from January to June or from July to December?

NOTE: You may have your students fill in a line graph of their own using the form on page 10.

 Graphs

Birthdays

In which month were you born?

Put a dot by the number on the graph. Connect the dots to finish your graph.

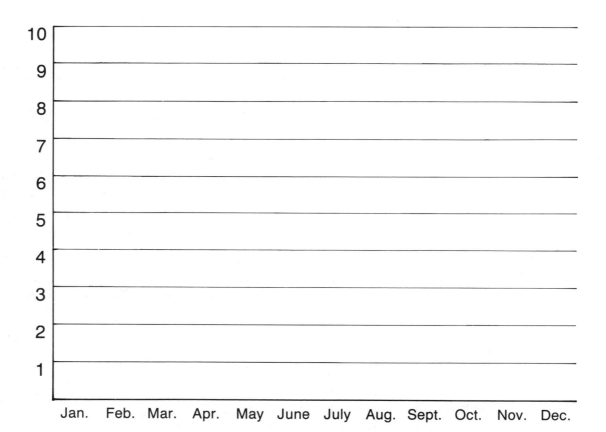

10
9
8
7
6
5
4
3
2
1

Jan. Feb. Mar. Apr. May June July Aug. Sept. Oct. Nov. Dec.

 Graphs

Make a class graph.

Take Me Out to the Ball Game

1. Brainstorm to list types of games played using a ball. List the names of the ball games (or draw pictures) on the chalkboard.
2. Reproduce the ball forms on the next page. (You will need to reproduce it several times.) Students select the picture that represents their favorite ball game, or you may have students draw pictures of the ball used in their favorite ball game. (Use 3'' X 3'' squares of paper.)
3. Make a large graph on butcher paper. Record the results by having students pin their pictures in the correct columns.

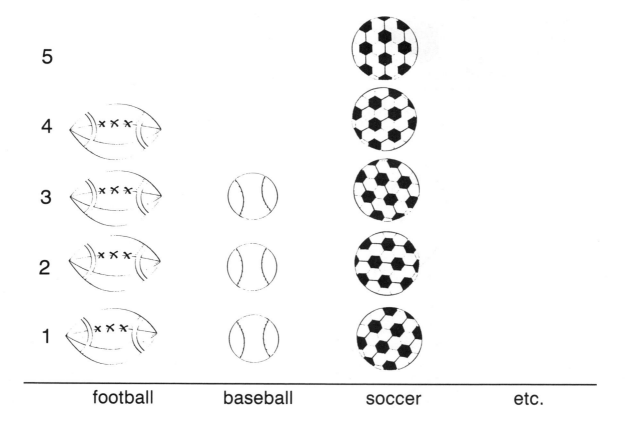

| | football | baseball | soccer | etc. |

4. Read the graph to find the answer to questions such as:
    a. Which ball games are listed on the graph?
    b. Which ball game was liked by the most boys and girls?
    c. Which ball game was liked by the least number of boys and girls?
    d. How many boys and girls chose _____?
    e. Was there a game listed that no one chose?

NOTE: You may have your students fill in their own graph using the form on page 13.

Patterns for "Ball" graph

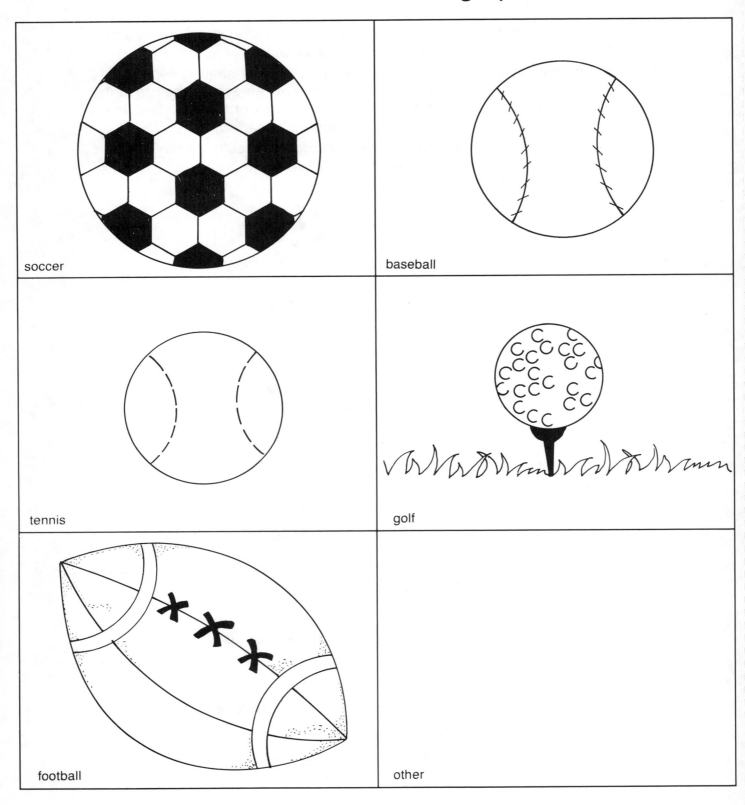

soccer

baseball

tennis

golf

football

other

12

Graphs

Take Me Out to the Ball Game

Which ball game do you like best?

Color one box for each ball game chosen. Start at one in each row.

	football	baseball	soccer	golf	tennis	other
15						
14						
13						
12						
11						
10						
9						
8						
7						
6						
5						
4						
3						
2						
1						

Graphs

Book Worms

1. Collecting information:

   Make a large graph on butcher paper. Display it in an area that your students can reach easily. Keep the graph to record library books read by the class for a specific amount of time (week, month, semester). After a student reads a library book he/she writes the title on a "book" (form is on the next page) and pins it to the graph. (This activity can be made more challenging by combining the books so that each "book" on the graph represents 2 or 10 books read.)

Books We Read in March

Week 1 GOOD BOOK GOOD BOOK GOOD BOOK

Week 2 GOOD BOOK GOOD BOOK GOOD BOOK GOOD BOOK GOOD BOOK GOOD BOOK

Week 3 GOOD BOOK GOOD BOOK GOOD BOOK GOOD BOOK

Week 4 GOOD BOOK GOOD BOOK GOOD BOOK GOOD BOOK GOOD BOOK

2. Read the graph to answer questions such as:

   a. How many books were read each week?

   week 1 _____   week 2 _____

   week 3 _____   week 4 _____

   b. In which week were the most books read?

   c. In which week were the fewest books read?

   d. Look at the book titles. Were any books read by more than one person? Which books?

   e. How many books were read in the whole month?

NOTE: You may have more able students make their own graph using the form on page 16. This can be a copy of the whole class graph or they may record their own reading for the month.

　　　　　　　　　　Graphs

Patterns for Book Worm Graph

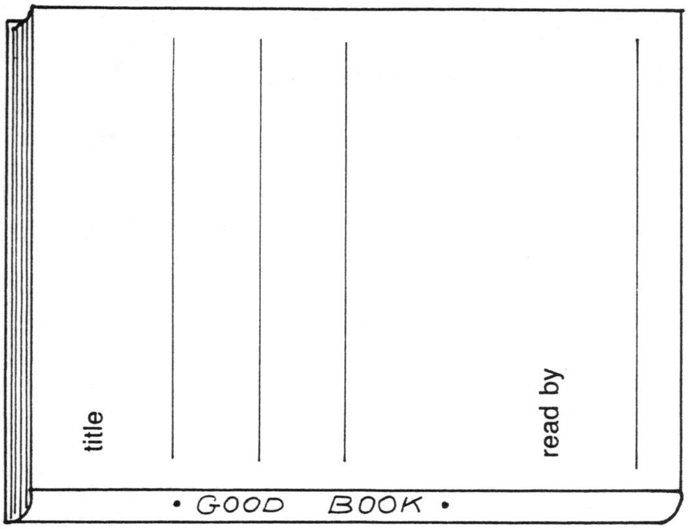

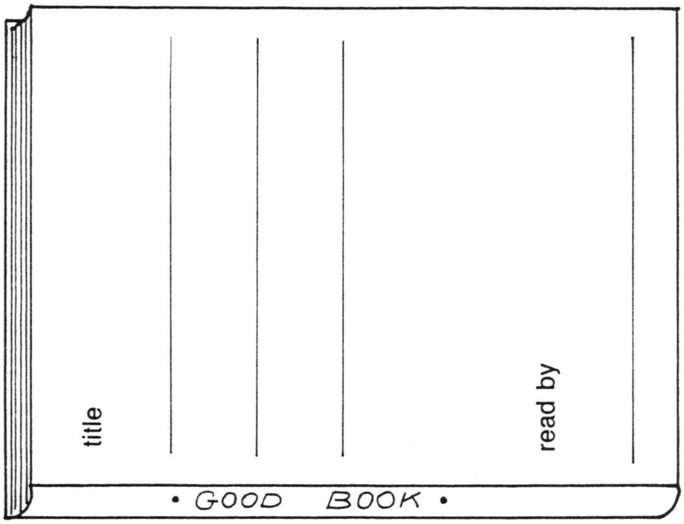

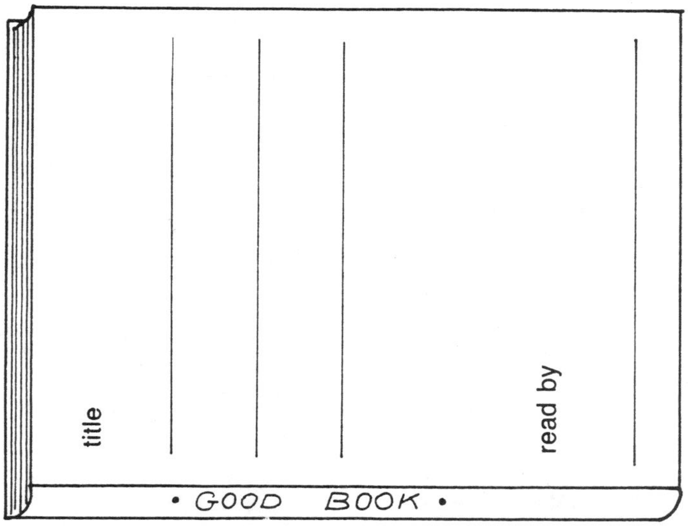

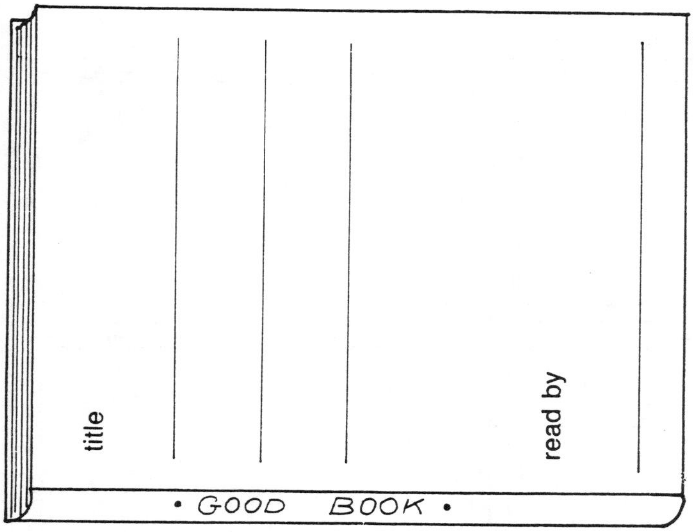

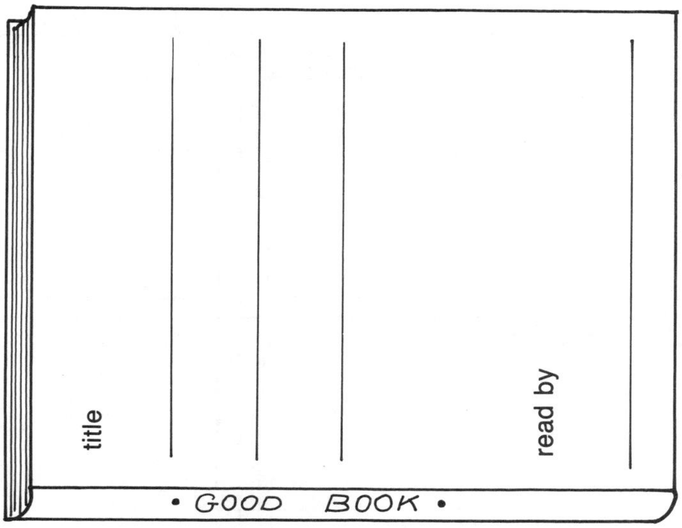

title   read by

• GOOD BOOK •

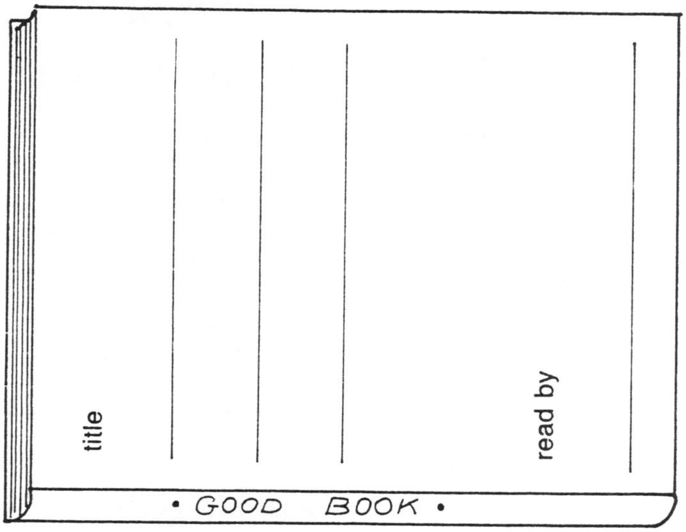

title   read by

• GOOD BOOK •

title   read by

• GOOD BOOK •

title   read by

• GOOD BOOK •

title   read by

• GOOD BOOK •

title   read by

• GOOD BOOK •

Graphs

Have students cut out and paste a picture for each book read in the correct row.

Books Read in _____
(month)
Each book on this graph means _____ books read.

Week 1	
Week 2	
Week 3	
Week 4	

GOOD BOOK GOOD BOOK GOOD BOOK GOOD BOOK GOOD BOOK GOOD BOOK

GOOD BOOK GOOD BOOK GOOD BOOK GOOD BOOK GOOD BOOK GOOD BOOK

Graphs

Ask 12 boys and girls, "Have you ever slept in a tent?"

Have the boys and girls put their names under the <u>yes</u> or <u>no.</u>

Yes	No

Answer these questions:
1. How many boys and girls have slept in a tent? _____
2. How many boys and girls have not slept in a tent? _____
3. Look at the names on your graph. Have more boys or girls slept in a tent? _____

17

Ask 12 children,
"Are you wearing sneakers right now?"

Have the boys and girls put their names under the yes or no.

yes
no

Answer these questions:
1. How many boys and girls were wearing sneakers? _____
2. How many boys and girls were not wearing sneakers? _____
3. Were more children wearing sneakers or not wearing sneakers? _____

                   Graphs

Hamburger? Pizza? Which is best?

1. Collect information:

   Ask 12 boys and girls, "Do you like pizza
   or hamburgers best?"

2. Record information:

   Color one box on your graph for each answer.
   (Start at number 1.)

3. Read your graph to answer these questions:

   a. How many boys and girls picked pizza? _____

   b. How many boys and girls picked hamburgers? _____

   c. Did most of the boys and girls like hamburgers or
      pizza best?   _____

12		
11		
10		
9		
8		
7		
6		
5		
4		
3		
2		
1		

pizza

hamburger

                                       Graphs

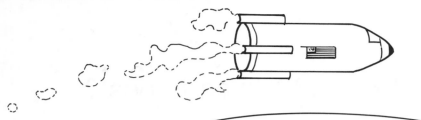

Space Travel

1. Collect information:

   Ask 12 boys and girls, "Would you go out into space if someone offered you a chance to ride in a space ship?"

2. Record information:

   Color one box on your graph for each answer.

3. Read your graph to answer these questions:

   a. How many boys and girls said yes? _____

   b. How many boys and girls said no? _____

   c. Did more children answer yes or no? _____

   d. Would you go into space if you had a chance? _____

	Yes, I would like to go into outer space.	No, I want to stay right here on Earth.
12		
11		
10		
9		
8		
7		
6		
5		
4		
3		
2		
1		

Bed Time

1. Collect information:

   Ask 12 boys and girls, "What time do you go to bed on a school night?"

2. Record information:

   Color one box on your graph for each answer.

3. Read your graph to answer these questions:

   a. What time do the most children go to bed? _____

   b. How many children go to bed at the same time you do? _____

   c. What is the latest time anyone you asked goes to bed? _____

   d. What is the earliest time anyone you asked goes to bed? _____

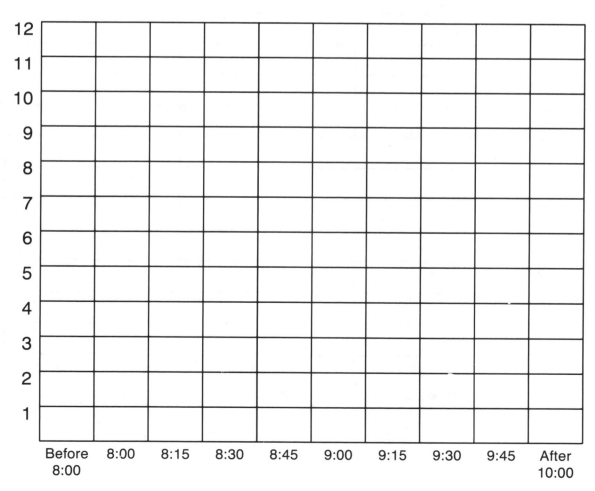

Let's Take a Vacation

1. Collect information:

   Ask 12 boys and girls, "Would you rather go to Disney World, Hawaii, or Alaska for a special vacation?"

2. Record information:

   Color one box on your graph for each answer.

3. Read your graph to answer these questions:

   a. How many boys and girls chose Alaska? _____

   b. How many boys and girls chose Hawaii? _____

   c. How many boys and girls chose Disney World? _____

   d. Which place was chosen the most times? _____

   e. Which place did the fewest children choose? _____

	Hawaii	Alaska	Disney World
12			
11			
10			
9			
8			
7			
6			
5			
4			
3			
2			
1			

Mitten Weather!

What color mittens did children wear to school?

Each (mitten) stands for five children.

red	🧤 🧤 🧤 🧤 🧤 🧤
brown	🧤 🧤 🧤 🧤
blue	🧤 🧤
yellow	🧤
green	🧤 🧤
black	🧤 🧤 🧤 🧤 🧤

Read the graph to answer these questions:

1. How many children wore _____ mittens?

    red _____   blue _____   black _____

    brown _____   green _____   yellow _____

2. What was the most popular color for mittens? _____

3. How many more children wore red than yellow? _____

4. Which two colors did the same number of children wear?

    _____   _____

5. How many children wore mittens all together? _____

23   Graphs

How do you help at home?

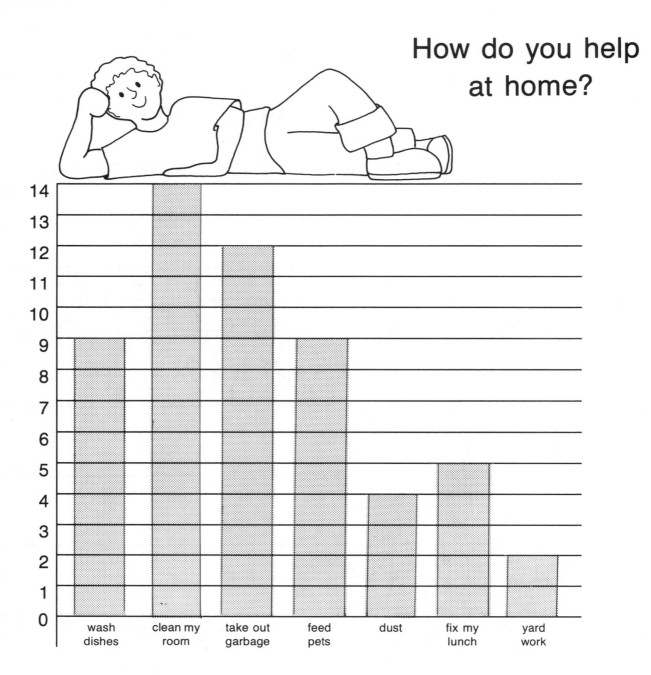

Read the graph to answer these questions:

1. Which job did the most children do? _____

2. Which job did the fewest children do? _____

3. How many children _____?

        take out garbage _____

        do yard work _____

        feed pets_____

        wash dishes _____

4. How many more clean their rooms than dust furniture? _____

5. Which two jobs did the same number of children do?

_____ _____

Who's the fastest?

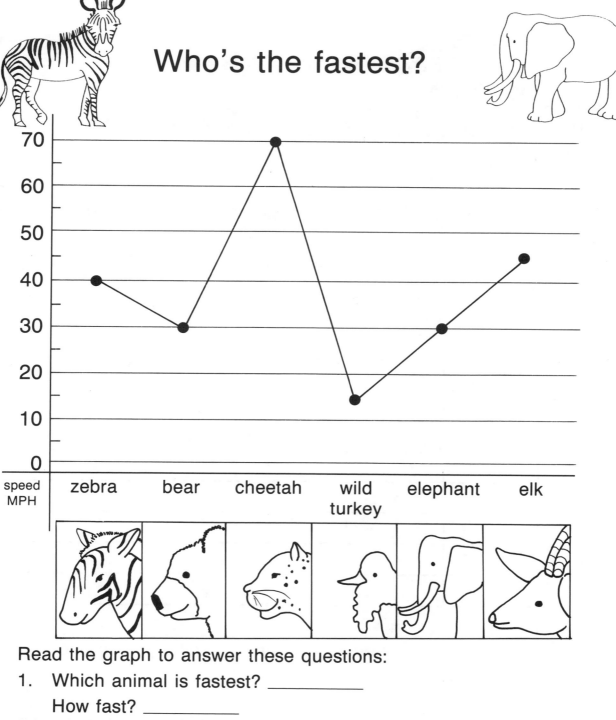

Read the graph to answer these questions:

1. Which animal is fastest? _____

   How fast? _____

2. Which animal is slowest? _____

   How slow? _____

3. Which two animals can run at the same speed?

   _____   _____

4. How much faster can an elk run than a zebra? _____

5. How much faster can the cheetah run than the elk? _____

25   Graphs

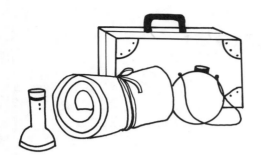

Summer Camp

What do you like to do best at summer camp?

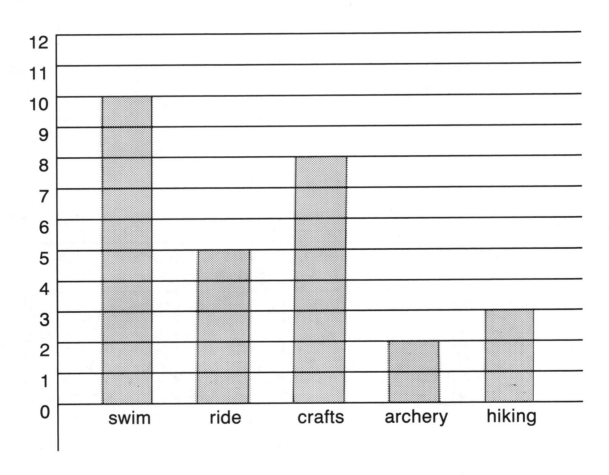

Read the graph to answer these questions about fun at summer camp:

1. How many boys and girls picked:

swimming _____   riding_____

crafts_____   archery_____

hiking _____

2. What was picked by the most boys and girls? _____

3. What was picked by the fewest boys and girls? _____

4. What would you pick? _____

                                       Graphs

Pets

What pets do you have?

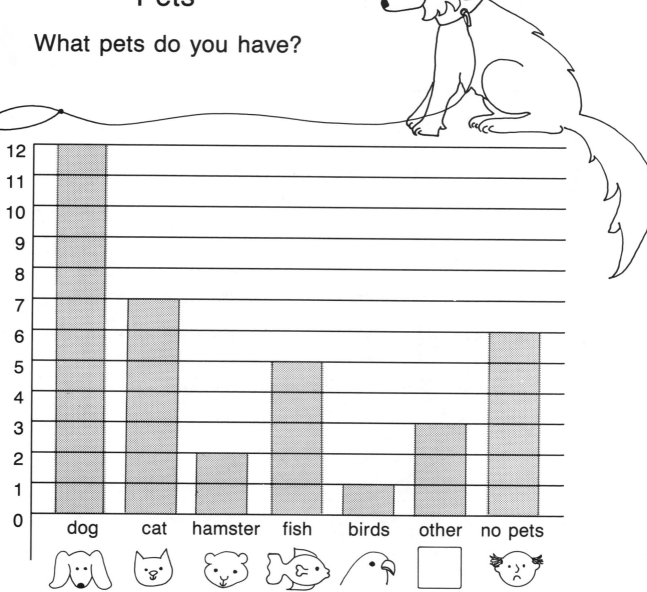

Read the graph to answer these questions about pets:

1. How many children have _____ for a pet?

    dogs _____   cats _____

    hamsters_____   fish_____

    birds _____   other _____

2. How many children did not have a pet? _____

3. Which pet did the most children have? _____

4. Which pet did the fewest children have? _____

Bonus:

Have many pets did the children have all together? _____

How long were dinosaurs?

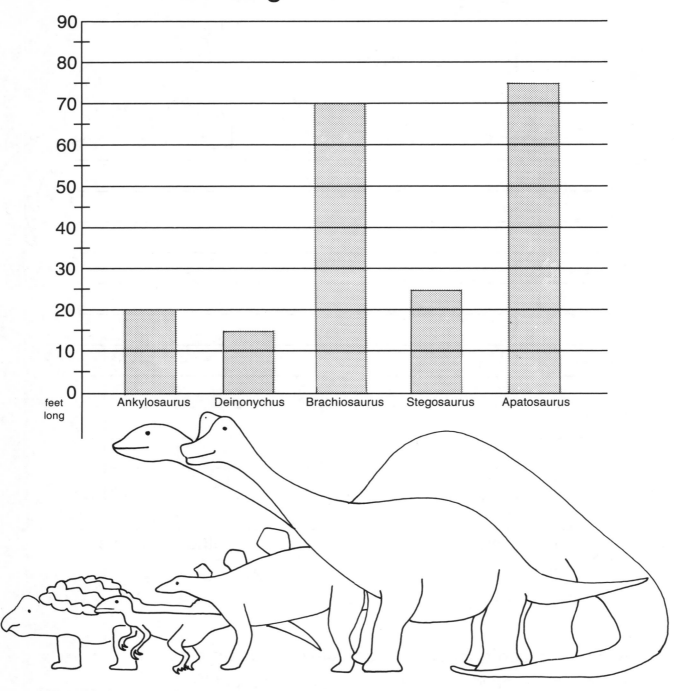

Read the graph to answer these questions:

1. Name the longest dinosaur. _____

    How long was it? _____

2. Name the shortest dinosaur. _____

    How long was it? _____

3. How much shorter was Ankylosaurus than Brachiosaurus? ____

4. How long were all five dinosaurs if you put them all together?

    _____

28   Graphs

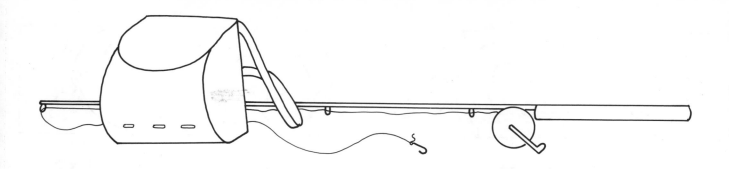

Going Fishing

How many fish did you catch?

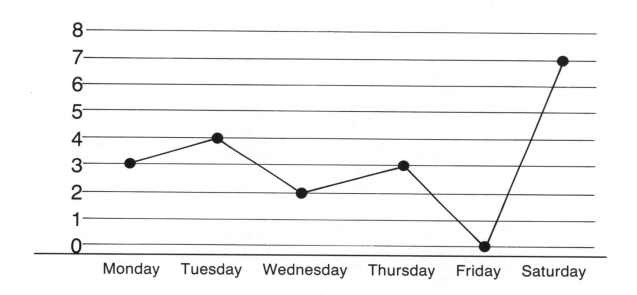

Read the line graph to answer these questions about fishing.

1. How many fish were caught on _____?

   Tuesday _____

   Thursday _____

   Saturday _____

2. Were more fish caught on Monday or Friday? _____

3. Were more fish caught on Tuesday or Saturday? _____

4. On which two days were the same amount of fish caught?

   _____   _____

Bonus: How many fish were caught all together? _____

How many boys and girls are in the third grade?

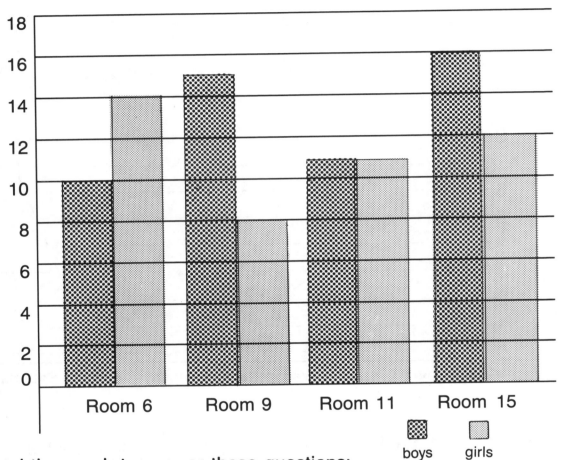

Read the graph to answer these questions:

1. How many boys are in _____?

        Room 6 _____   Room 9 _____

        Room 11_____   Room 15_____

2. How many girls are in _____?

        Room 6 _____   Room 9 _____

        Room 11_____   Room 15_____

3. Which room has the same number of boys and girls? _____

4. Which rooms have more boys than girls? _____

Bonus: How many boys all together? _____

        How many girls all together? _____

        How many children in third grade? _____

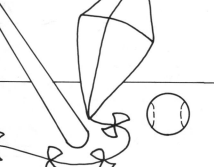

Toys for Sale

Come to the big five-day sale at Toy Town.

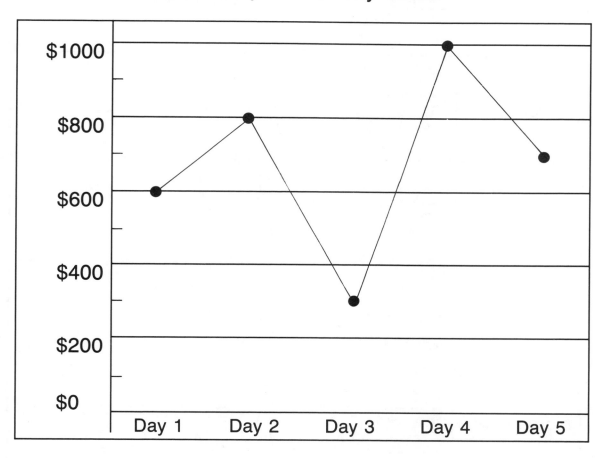

Read the graph to answer these questions:

1. How much was sold on _____?

        Day 3 _____

        Day 1 _____

        Day 5 _____

2. On what day was the greatest amount sold? _____

3. On what day was the smallest amount sold? _____

4. How much more was sold on day 4 than on day 1? _____

Bonus: How much was sold all together? _____

How many people live here?

Each 🧍 equals 10,000 people.

Madera	🧍🧍🧍
Cooperville	🧍🧍🧍🧍
West Park	🧍🧍🧍🧍
Morgantown	🧍🧍🧍🧍🧍🧍

Read the graph to answer these questions:

1. How much does 🧍 equal? _____
2. How much does 🧍 equal? _____
3. Which town has the most people? _____
4. Which town has the fewest people? _____
5. How many more people live in Morgantown than Madera? _____
6. How many more people live in West Park than in Cooperville? _____

     Graphs